Comptroller of the Currency
Administrator of National Banks

Bank Dealer Activities

Comptroller's Handbook
(Section 204)

Narrative and Procedures - March 1990

Other Income Producing Activities

Bank Dealer Activities (Section 204)

Table of Contents

Bank Dealer
Activities (Section 204)   Introduction

A bank operates as a securities dealer when it underwrites, trades, or deals in securities. Those activities are usually administered in a separately identifiable trading department; however, the lack of such a department does not preclude a bank's involvement in dealer activities. If a repetitive pattern of short-term purchases and sales demonstrates that the bank holds itself out to other dealers or investors as a securities dealer, the bank is trading, regardless of what department or section of the bank processes the transactions.

The authority under which a bank may engage in securities trading and underwriting is found in 12 USC 24. That authority is restricted by limitations on percentage holding of classes of securities as found in 12 CFR 1.3. That regulation allows banks to deal in, underwrite, purchase, and sell Type I securities without limit, and Type II securities limited to 10 percent of its capital and unimpaired surplus. Banks are prohibited from underwriting or dealing in Type III securities for their own accounts.

There are three major types of securities transactions in which banks are involved. First, the bank may buy and sell securities on behalf of a customer. Those are agency transactions in which the agent (bank) assumes no substantial risk and is compensated by a prearranged commission or fee. Second, as a dealer, the bank buys and sells securities for its own account. That is termed a principal transaction because the bank is acting as a principal, buying or selling qualified securities through its own inventory and absorbing whatever market gain or loss is made on the transaction. The third type of securities transaction frequently executed by banks is a contemporaneous, "riskless," principal trade. The dealer buys and sells qualified securities as a principal, with the purchase and sale originating almost simultaneously. Exposure to market risks is limited by the brief period of actual ownership and profits result from dealer initiated mark-up, the difference between the purchase and sale prices.

Bank dealers' securities transactions involve customers and other securities dealers. The word customer, as used in this section, means an investor. Transactions with other dealers are not considered customer transactions unless the dealer is buying or selling for investment purposes.

The following subsections include general descriptions of significant areas of bank trading and underwriting activities.

Government Securities Trading

The government securities market is dominated by a group of dealer firms and banks that make up the Association of Primary Dealers in Government Securities. These specialists make an over-the-counter market in most government and federal agency securities. As market makers, they quote bid and ask prices and several of them publish daily quotation sheets. Prices for all government securities transactions are negotiated on the basis of those publicly quoted bid and ask prices. The difference between the bid and ask prices is usually smaller for actively traded short-term securities than for less active long-term issues. The spread between bid and ask prices also can vary because of the size of a given purchase and sale.

Government security trading inventories are generally held with the objective of making short-term gains through market appreciation and dealer initiated markups. The size of a transaction, the dealer efforts extended and the nature of the security are common factors that affect the mark-up differential. Mark-ups on government securities generally range between one and four thirty-seconds of a point. Long maturity issues or derivative products may have higher mark-ups.

The market risk inherent in U.S. government trading portfolios should be controlled by bank policy. Standards should be established to limit the total security inventory and the amount of securities with similar yield or maturity characteristics. Limits imposed by policy should include commitments to purchase new governments on a "when issued" basis.

Payments for and deliveries of U.S. government and most agency securities are settled on the business day following the trade. Government dealers and customers can negotiate same day or delayed settlement for special situations, but the industry recognizes regular-way settlement as occurring on the trade date plus one business day.

Due Bills

If a bank sells, collects the proceeds, and fails to deliver the security, a due bill exists in favor of the paying customer. To satisfy their disclosure obligations under the federal securities laws, banks are required to make full written disclosure, on a timely basis, to affected customers of all material facts and circumstances concerning due bills. Under no circumstances should a bank send a due bill customer any document that has the potential to mislead the customer. Failure to inform customers or use of misleading documents about due bill transactions could be considered a violation of the antifraud provisions of federal securities laws. Due bills outstanding more than 3 business days are subject to demand deposit reserve requirements, unless the due bill is fully collateralized by securities similar to, and with a market value at least equal to, those securities that are the subject of the due bill transaction. A security is similar if it is of the same type and of comparable maturity to that purchased by the customer. (For example, if a U.S. Treasury bill is the subject of a due bill transaction, collateralization should be provided in the form of other U.S. Treasury bills with a market value at least equal to that of the security sold.) A pool of securities may be used to collateralize due bills as long as the type, maturity, and market value requirements are met. Acceptable uses for due bills should be defined by policy.

Due bills can occur in the sale of any bank asset. In such circumstances, the above standards apply. Due bills occur most frequently as a result of U.S. government securities dealer activity. If the bank has accepted funds for U.S. government securities purchases, but has not placed the order for the purchase by the next business day, then the bank must provide notice to the customer and deposit funds into an account for the customer. Alternatively, the bank can implement the "buy-in" provisions of the Government Securities Act.

Clearance

Securities clearance services for the bulk of U.S. government and federal agency security transactions are provided by the Federal Reserve as part of its telegraphic securities transfer system. The various Federal Reserve banks will wire transfer most government securities between the book entry safekeeping accounts of the seller and buyer. The Federal Reserve's systems also are used to facilitate security borrowings, loans, and pledges.

Most bank dealers participate in the government securities market by engaging in inter-dealer trading and transacting customer orders as both principal and agent. Banks also frequently deal directly with various government fiscal agents in acquiring new issue securities.

Short-Sales

Another area of U.S. government security activity involves short-sale transactions. A short-sale is the sale and delivery of a security that the seller does not own. It is accomplished by borrowing the security for delivery. The borrowed security is collateralized by an appropriate amount of a similar security. Carrying charges on borrowed government securities are generally equivalent to 0.5 percent per annum of their par value and are deducted from the short-sale and purchase spread to determine net profit.

Short-sales are conducted to accommodate customer orders, to obtain funds by leveraging existing assets, to hedge the market risk of other assets, or with the expectation that the market price of the sold security will decline sufficiently to allow the bank to complete the transaction by purchasing an equivalent security at a later date and a lower price.

Arbitrage

Arbitrage is the coordinated purchase and sale of two securities in which there is a relative market imbalance. The objective of such activity is to obtain earnings, by taking advantage of changing yield spreads. Arbitrage opportunities take many forms and can exist whenever segments of the securities markets are subject to a yield variance.

When executing an arbitraged short-sale, trades often choose to buy securities pledged against borrowed securities in a transaction, simultaneous with the short-sale, thus the two transactions offset one another. The actual cash outlay for acquiring the collateral is limited to the difference between the short-sale proceeds and the cost of the purchased security. That serves as a hedge because if the market price of the short-sale security increases, the purchased security can be delivered to the lender of the security with a minimum of loss. The potential for profits on price declines remains unchanged, but the risk of loss resulting from price increases is hedged.

Exposure on arbitrage and/or short-sales should be closely monitored for compliance with predetermined objectives. Risk should be controlled by point spread limits coordinated with "stop loss" buy or sell provisions and by guidelines on the length of time a short position can remain uncovered.

Money Market Trading

Aside from short-term securities, banks customarily trade a substantial volume of other money market instruments. A sound money market trading policy recognizes the need for a qualitative analysis of the issuers of instruments in which the bank regularly deals. Credit approvals should be obtained prior to effecting repurchase transactions or trading in a corporation's commercial paper or in another bank's CDs, acceptances or federal funds, and reviews should be conducted on a regular schedule.

Banks dealing in money market instruments are subject to a number of legal restrictions. The sale of federal funds by a national bank to an affiliate acting as principal is limited under 12 USC 371(c). The acquisition, as principal, of a CD issued by an affiliate also is subject to 12 USC 371(c) limitations. Under 12 CFR 217.4(d), a bank may not purchase its own CDs for its own account.

Federal Funds

Dealer banks usually provide federal funds clearing services to their correspondent banks. Buys are executed on a daily basis, usually under a continuing service contract that does not specify maturity and amount and does not require advance notice for termination. Generally, the interest rate on such a contract is adjusted daily. The arrangement is analogous to a series of one-day transactions with sales made to approved buyers at the highest available rate. Transactions are customarily unsecured.

Banks also deal in longer maturity money market investments with fixed rates of return such as, bankers' acceptances, commercial paper, negotiable certificates of deposit (CDs), and Eurodollar CDs. Each class of money market instrument has specialized characteristics.

Bankers' Acceptances

Bankers' acceptances are an obligation of the acceptor bank and an indirect obligation of the drawer. They are normally secured by rights to the goods being financed and are available in a wide variety of principal amounts. Maturities are generally less than 9 months. Acceptances are priced like Treasury bills, with a discount figured for the actual number of days to maturity based on a 360-day year.

Commercial Paper

Banks also trade commercial paper issued by corporations to finance short-term credit needs. Commercial paper is a security in the form of an unsecured promissory note with a maturity of less than nine months. Actively traded commercial paper is ordinarily issued in denominations of $100,000, $250,000, $500,000, or $1 million. Smaller denominations may be issued by obligors whose commercial paper is less actively traded. Commercial paper is customarily backed by unused bank credit lines sufficient to repay the liability. Major commercial paper issuers are rated by Moody's, Standard and Poor's and other services.

Commercial paper may be issued as an interest-bearing instrument or at a discount. Market trades are priced at a current yield, net of accrued interest due the seller or, if the commercial paper was issued at a discount, at a discount figured for the actual number of days to maturity based on a 360-day year.

The sale of commercial paper issued by bank affiliates must be conducted in a manner that conforms to legal restrictions and avoids conflicts of interest. Principal trades are restricted by 12 USC 371(c). Agent sales should be made to sophisticated investors only, and in denominations of $25,000 or more. When "as agent" sales of affiliate commercial paper are conducted, the agent must ensure that the purchaser is fully informed and aware of the nature of the transaction. Each certificate and confirmation should disclose the facts that the commercial paper is not a deposit and is not insured by the Federal Deposit Insurance Corporation.

Certificates of Deposit

Negotiable CDs issued by money center banks are actively traded in denominations of $100,000 to $1 million. Interest is generally calculated on a 360-day year and paid at maturity. Secondary market prices are computed based on current yield, net of accrued interest due the seller. Eurodollar CDs trade like domestic CDs except their yields are usually higher and their maturities often longer.

Money market instruments trade with the same day or one-day settlement. Publicly quoted yields or dollar prices are usually based on round lot trades of

$1 million, except for commercial paper which trades in round lots of $250,000. Odd lot prices may vary, but because of the large dollar volume of most trades, the percentage spread between the acquisition cost and sale price is characteristically modest.

Bank management should attempt to minimize market risk by establishing a maximum holding limit for each class of money market principal. Policy guidelines also should establish concentration limits for money market instruments issued by a single obligor. Such limits should include commitments.

Offsetting Repurchase Transactions

Another money market activity encountered in dealer banks involves resale and repurchase agreements. Money market instruments or securities, usually U.S. government securities, are purchased under an agreement to resell, "reverse repo," and resold under an agreement to repurchase, "repo."

Banks purchase "reverse repos" to finance the U.S. government securities inventory of other dealers or mortgage bankers who have originated pools of mortgages to back federal housing agency securities. Repos are sold to bank customers in lieu of certificates of deposits. Banks employ repos of government securities as borrowing substitutes and, as deposit substitutes because they are exempt from Regulation Q interest limitations and from Regulation D reserve requirements. Repos are generally a less expensive method of acquiring source funds. Customers find them attractive because interest can be paid on repos having maturities of less than 30 days and because customer funds are collateralized by the security underlying the repurchase transaction.

The rate of interest received and paid is generally dictated by prevailing market rates. Profits are based on a modest positive spread between interest earned and interest paid. A bank dealer may attempt to improve that modest profit by increasing the volume of such transactions, using the proceeds to finance or pyramid the acquisition of "reverse repos" or securities to be used in additional "repo" arrangements.

A common dealer strategy is to vary resale and repurchase maturities in anticipation of interest rate movements. If an upward rate trend is expected, the dealer will attempt to lock-in cheaper source funds at the current low rate by negotiating longer maturities for "repos" and shorter maturities for "reverse repos." Conversely, if interest rates are expected to decline, the bank attempts to negotiate longer maturity "reverse repos" to ensure continuing higher earnings, while negotiating shorter maturity "repos" to take advantage of cheaper future source funds.

Care should be taken to limit the bank's exposure by instituting policy guidelines that:

- Limit the aggregate amounts of "reverse repo" and "repo" accounts.

- Specify acceptable amounts of funds for unmatched or extended maturity transactions.

- Determine maximum time gaps for unmatched maturity transactions and minimally acceptable interest rate spreads for various maturity agreements.

The examiner must remember that "reverse repo" agreements are merely another form of secured lending. Policy guidelines should limit the amount of money extended to one or related firms through the use of "reverse repos." Firms selling securities under such agreements should provide the bank with corporate resolutions stating the names and limits of the persons who are authorized to commit the firm and provide current financial statements. The firm should then be subjected to credit review. Board or committee credit approvals should be updated periodically.

Collateral coverage on "reverse repo" arrangements should be controlled by procedures similar to the safeguards used to control any type of liquid collateral. Funds should not be paid until specified types of properly assigned or registered securities are delivered into the bank's physical custody or to an independent safekeeping agent. They should only be advanced against pre-determined collateral margins or discounts. The percentage of advance on collateral margin or the extent of discount from the collateral's market value should be determined by:

- The type of security pledged as collateral.

- The maturity of the collateral.

- The historic and anticipated price volatility of the collateral.

- The maturity of the "reverse repo" agreement.

The minimum acceptable market value coverage of all but short-term government securities collateral is usually considered to be 102 percent of the funds advanced. Collateral margins or discounts should be supported by maintenance agreements that require the selling firm to maintain sufficient collateral coverage over the life of the "reverse repo" agreement.

Those agreements should permit margin calls before market declines significantly erode margin coverage. The market value of collateral should also be frequently checked to the bid side of the market to determine compliance with margin and maintenance requirements.

Procedures should also ensure that collateral for "repo" transactions is properly controlled. Because of the characteristic high volume of activity, collateral securing a "repo" could be pledged to more than one customer. That type of double financing would be an unsecured borrowing and could also be grounds for legal action under the Securities and Exchange Commission's antifraud provisions.

Trading and Underwriting of Municipal Securities

The Securities Acts Amendments of 1975 extended a comprehensive network of federal regulation to the municipal securities markets. Municipal securities brokers and dealers are required to register with the Securities and Exchange Commission (SEC). The Act also created a separate, self-regulatory body, the Municipal Securities Rulemaking Board (MSRB), to formulate working rules for the regulation of the municipal securities industry. The Office of the Comptroller of the Currency (OCC) is required, by statute, to enforce those rules as they apply to national banks.

A bank or, at its option, a separately identifiable department "engaged in the business of buying and selling municipal securities," must register with the SEC as a municipal securities dealer. A bank that buys and sells municipal securities for its investment portfolio or in a fiduciary capacity is not generally considered a dealer. Under SEC guidelines, a bank must register if it is involved in:

- Underwriting or participating in a syndicate or joint account for the purpose of purchasing securities;

- Maintaining a trading account or carrying dealer inventory; or

- Advertising or listing itself as a dealer in trade publications or otherwise holding itself out to other dealers or investors as a dealer.

Separately Identifiable Department

MSRB rule G-1 defines a "separately identifiable department or division of a bank" involved in municipal securities dealing as a unit, under the supervision of officers designated by the bank's board of directors, responsible for municipal securities dealer activities, that maintains separate or separately extractable records, and performs any of the following:

- Underwrites, trades, and/or sells municipal securities.

- Offers financial advisory and consultant services for issuers in connection with the issuance of municipal securities.

- Provides processing and clearing services for municipal securities.

- Offers research and investment advice on municipal securities.

- Communicates in other ways with public investors in municipal securities.

- Maintains records of the activities described above.

Those standards from the SEC and the MSRB should serve as guidelines for the examiner in determining if a bank is engaged in municipal securities dealer activities.

Professional Qualification Standards

MSRB rules impose standards that prohibit transactions in municipal securities unless the dealer and all associated persons are properly qualified.

Those standards include minimum supervisory staffing requirements for dealers.

A bank with 10 or fewer people in its municipal securities dealer operations must have at least one "municipal securities principal." A municipal securities principal is an individual engaged in the management, direction, and supervision of municipal securities activities and in the training of municipal securities personnel. Banks with more than 10 people in their municipal securities dealer operations must have at least two municipal securities principals.

A municipal securities representative is defined as a person engaged in a municipal securities dealer activity in other than in a supervisory or clerical capacity. Generally, all municipal securities principals and representatives are required to pass a qualification examination. There are certain exceptions to that requirement based upon prior qualification or history or experience in a field closely related to the municipal securities business.

A qualified person who ceases his or her association with a municipal securities broker or dealer for 2 or more years must take and pass an appropriate examination before again effecting transactions in municipal securities. An individual entering the municipal securities business must serve a 90-day apprenticeship before transacting such business with the public.

There are some blanket disqualifications under statute, and persons or firms who are subject to restrictions because of regulatory disciplinary action may also be prohibited from transacting municipal securities business.

Every bank or bank department registered as a municipal securities dealer must maintain a record identifying each associated person, the type of functions he or she performs and whether he or she was exempt or has taken and passed a qualifying examination.

Municipal securities dealers must obtain information on the identity, education, past employment, and disciplinary history of all associated persons. When an individual becomes associated with a municipal securities dealer, the dealer must verify that information by contacting each person that employed the individual during the preceding 3 years. The information must be corrected by the associated person if it becomes inaccurate or incomplete. 12 CFR 10.4 requires that national bank municipal securities dealers submit to the OCC on Form MSD-4 certain information on municipal securities principals or representatives prior to their association. If any such information becomes materially inaccurate or incomplete, the applicant must furnish the correct or missing information to the bank. The bank, within 10 days of receiving such information, must submit it to the OCC. Within 30 days after an association ceases, bank management must prepare Form MSD-5 explaining the reason for the termination and file the form with OCC.

Recordkeeping Rules

MSRB rule G-8 describes the records to be maintained by each registered municipal securities dealer for all municipal security transactions. The rule requires the following records:

- "Blotters," journals, or other records of original entry, containing an itemized daily record of all purchases, sales, receipts, and deliveries of municipal securities; all receipts and disbursements of cash; and all other debits and credits pertaining to municipal securities transactions.

- Account records for each customer account. The bank dealer's account should reflect all purchases, sales, receipts, and deliveries of municipal securities; all receipts and disbursements of cash; and all other debits and credits relating to the account.

- Securities records, showing all positions in each municipal security held for the bank's own account, the location of those securities and the position to short sold securities. Short positions should be so designated.

- Subsidiary records, consisting of ledgers or other records which reflect municipal securities in transfer, those sent to be validated, borrowed, or loaned, and transactions not completed by settlement date (fails).

- Records of all written or oral options to sell (put options) or repurchase municipal securities in which the bank has a direct or indirect interest or which the bank has guaranteed.

- A memorandum of each agency order and accompanying instructions, terms, or conditions. The record should indicate the account for which the order was entered, the date and time of receipt of the order, price at which it was executed, date, and time of execution. If an agency order is canceled by a customer, the records should show the terms, conditions, and date and time of cancellation.

- A memorandum of each principal transaction in municipal securities, showing the price, date, and time of execution. In the event such a purchase or sale involves a customer, a record of his or her order should also be maintained, showing the date and time of receipt, the terms and conditions of the order, and the name or other designation of the account in which it was entered.

- Records on each syndicate or similar account formed for the purchase of municipal securities must be maintained by a managing underwriter designated by those accounts.

- A copy for municipal securities of all confirmations of purchase and sale, notices of debits and credits, cash, and other items.

- Customer account information, consisting of a record of each customer's name and address, whether he or she is of legal age, tax identification or social security number, occupation, and name and address of employer.

- Customer information required by rule G-19 such as financial background, tax status, investment objectives, or other information used or necessary when making recommendations to a customer.

- Records of all written customer complaints and notations of the bank's actions concerning those grievances.

Rule G-8 does not require bank dealers to maintain records in a specific manner. Required information may be set forth on a single record or a group of secondary records, provided that it is clearly and accurately reflected and is sufficient for audit or examination purposes. For example, account records may be kept in several different formats to satisfy the requirements, such as separate ledgers for each customer or copies of confirmations and other source documents filed by customer name. In either case, the required information must appear. Groups of secondary records must be available for immediate inspection by examiners and to facilitate proper internal supervisory control to be effective for examination purposes.

Under rule G-8, a bank lacking securities clearance services does not have to maintain required records, provided that they are kept by the person performing those services. However, if the bank's clearing agent is not a clearing broker or dealer (registered broker or dealer), the bank must ensure that the records are maintained and preserved correctly. All clearing agent arrangements must be approved by the OCC.

MSRB rule G-9 lists various time frames for preservation of required municipal security records. Records must be maintained in an easily accessible place for at least 2 years and thereafter be available to OCC examiners within a reasonable period of time. They may be retained in any manner provided the bank has adequate facilities for retrieval and for production of readable copies. If records are maintained on microfilm, electronic tape, or similar medium, duplicates must be stored separately for the time periods required by the rule.

MSRB rule G-10 requires the delivery of an "investor brochure" to a customer upon receipt of a complaint by the customer.

Sales of New Issue Municipal Securities During the Underwriting Period

MSRB Rule G-11 addresses the operation of underwriting syndicates.

Every bank dealer submitting an order to a syndicate to purchase securities must disclose if the order is being submitted for the dealer's own account or for the account of related municipal securities portfolios, i.e., bank-owned or affiliated bank portfolios or trust portfolios. Every bank dealer submitting a group order (an order for the account of all syndicate members on a pro rata basis according to each member's interest in the syndicate) must disclose the identity of the person for whom the order is submitted.

Every bank dealer functioning as the senior manager of a syndicate must disclose, in writing:

- The identity of each related portfolio for which an order was submitted, including the par amounts and maturities so allocated.

- The identity of each person submitting a group order to which securities have been allocated.

- A summary of the allocation of securities to other orders, including any order confirmed at a price other than the original list price that indicates par value and maturity.

Every syndicate must establish the priority of different types of orders for purchase of syndicate securities, if this priority can be changed and the procedures for doing so. Prior to offering securities, the syndicate manager must, in writing, communicate to syndicate members:

- The priority of orders.

- Procedures for changing order priority.

- That the manager is permitted to allocate securities on a case-by-case basis.

- Whether orders may be confirmed prior to the end of the period during which orders are being solicited. Any changes in procedures governing the priority of various types of orders have to be promptly communicated in writing by the syndicate manager to members.

At or before final settlement of the syndicate, the senior manager must furnish members with an itemized statement setting forth the nature and amount of expenses incurred for the syndicate.

Uniform Practices

Rule G-12 establishes uniform industry practices for the processing, clearance, and settlement of transactions in municipal securities between brokers and dealers. The rule does not apply to transactions with customers. Provisions of the rule cover:

- Uniform settlement dates.

- Dealer-to-dealer confirmation procedures and content.

- Reporting and resolving unrecognized transactions.

- Acceptable methods of delivery and payment.

- Procedures for rejections and reclamations.

- Close-out procedures.

- Time periods for the return of good faith deposits and the settlement of syndicate accounts. Sections of the rule addressing dealer confirmations, the return of good faith deposits, the settlement of syndicate accounts, and the distribution of credits on designated orders must be observed as written. Other requirements may be altered by mutual agreement between a buyer and seller.

The term "settlement date" means the day used in price and interest calculations and shall be the delivery date unless altered by mutual consent of the parties to a trade. Settlement date for "cash" transactions is the trade date. "Regular way" settlement date is the fifth business day following the trade date. "When, as and if issued" (WI) settlement date is a date agreed to by both parties. Buying and selling dealers are required to exchange confirmations within one business day after the trade date. Dealer confirmations must include certain minimum information as specified in MSRB rule G12. The exchange of confirmations is required so that they can be compared for discrepancies. If discrepancies are discovered either by the selling dealer or buying dealer, the rule specifies what steps must be taken to resolve them. If material discrepancies are not resolved, the transaction may be canceled by either party.

A purchasing dealer may reject delivery of securities on a properly confirmed trade if the selling dealer fails to make "good delivery." The rule specifies what constitutes good delivery.

Once delivery is accepted and payment made, a buyer or seller can still reverse the trade by "reclamation," i.e., the return by the receiving party of securities previously accepted for delivery, or a demand by the delivering party for the return of delivered securities. Securities may be reclaimed by either party if information is discovered which, if known at the time of delivery, would have prevented good delivery.

Reclamation or rejection of a securities transaction can only be accomplished by written notice and within a certain time period after the transaction.

In addition to reclamation and rejection of a securities transaction, rule G-12 provides for "close-out" procedures. A close-out can occur in instances when a seller has made good delivery which is rejected by a purchaser, or when a purchaser fails to receive good delivery of a confirmed securities transaction. Certain notice requirements must be met to effect a close-out under rule G-12.

Rule G-12 also addresses the settlement of syndicate accounts as follows:

- Good faith deposits must be returned to members of a syndicate within 2 business days of settlement with the issuer or, in the event the syndicate is not successful in purchasing the issue, within 2 business days following return of the deposit from the issuer.

- Final settlement must be within 60 days following delivery of the securities by the manager to the members.

- Credits designated by a customer which are due to a syndicate member must be distributed by the municipal securities broker or dealer handling the order within 30 days following delivery of the securities to the customer.

Quotations Relating to Municipal Securities and Reports of Sales and Purchases

MSRB Rule G-13 applies to all municipal securities quotations disseminated by or on behalf of a bank dealer. For purposes of the rule, the term "quotations" means any bid for and offer of municipal securities, or a request for bids for or offers of municipal securities.

The rule prohibits a bank municipal securities dealer from disseminating quotations unless the bank is prepared to buy or sell securities according to stated conditions. Nominal quotations given merely as an indication of price, and solely for informational purposes, must be clearly identified as nominal quotations when given. No bank dealer may issue any quotation unless, in the dealer's best judgment, it represents the fair market value for the securities.

If a bank dealer is a member of a joint account formed to purchase or sell securities, quotations by the dealer for joint account securities must be joint account quotations.

MSRB Rule G-14 provides that a bank dealer may only disseminate reports of purchases and sales of municipal securities if it believes that a purchase or sale actually occurred.

Customer Confirmations

Confirmations must be sent or given to customers at or before completion of a transaction in municipal securities. The timing and content of those confirmations is governed by MSRB Rule G-15. Customer confirmations must contain:

- All of the information required to be disclosed on dealer confirmations except concession data.

- The time of execution of a trade or a statement that the time will be furnished upon written request of the customer.

- Disclosure of capacity as principal, or as agent for the customer, for a person other than the customer, or for both the customer and another person.

- For transactions effected on the basis of dollar price, both the dollar price and the lowest of the resulting yield to premium call, par option or maturity.

Customer confirmations of agency transactions must disclose:

- The amount and source of any commission, fee, or other remuneration received or to be received by a bank dealer.

- The name of the contra-party or a statement that the information will be furnished upon request. Requests for information required to be disclosed by G-15 must be responded to within 5 business days of receipt of a request. When a transaction takes place 30 days prior to receipt of a request, a response must be made within 15 business days.

Standards of Fair Practice

MSRB Rule G-17 requires bank dealers to deal fairly with all persons and not engage in any deceptive, dishonest, or unfair practices.

MSRB Rule G-18, "Execution of Transactions," requires bank dealers executing transactions as agent for a customer to make a reasonable effort to obtain a price that is fair and reasonable relative to the prevailing market for all customers. The rule also pertains to a bank dealer acting in a "broker's broker" capacity, i.e., effecting transactions for other brokers or dealers on a regular basis. The capacity in which a bank dealer acts is determined by instructions from the customer. If the customer intends the bank dealer to buy (or sell) a security for the customer without the bank dealer actually being the seller (or buyer), the bank would be the customer's agent. A practice has developed among some bank dealers to consider the bank's capacity as agent for the customer in all securities transactions that are ineligible for a bank dealer to deal in as principle and to consider the bank's capacity as principal in all transactions in eligible securities. This is an improper practice and should be criticized. The fairness and reasonableness of a price may be determined by comparing trade prices to independently established market prices. Independent market prices often may be observed merely by looking at the other side of a "riskless" principal sale or by noting the prices of contemporaneous principal sales of the same security. If independent price quotes cannot be obtained, trade value should be tested by comparative yield analysis. Reasonable mark-ups and/or fees on "riskless" principal or agent sales of securities purchased from dealers seldom exceed the amount of dealer concession. For "riskless" principal sales of securities purchased from a customer, a reasonable mark-up seldom exceeds 2 percent and rarely exceeds 4 percent of the market value of the security.

MSRB Rule G-19, "Suitability of Recommendations and Transactions: Discretionary Accounts," requires that the bank dealer have all customer information required by MSRB Rule G-8(a)(xi) and knowledge of or inquire about the customer's financial background, tax status, investment objectives, and any other similar information before completion of a municipal transaction with a customer. A municipal securities dealer cannot recommend a municipal securities transaction unless, after reasonable inquiry, it has reasonable grounds to believe and does believe that the transaction is suitable in light of customer information provided, knowledge of the customer, or information available from the issuer of the security. If the municipal securities dealer determines that a municipal transaction would not be suitable for a customer and so informs the customer, the dealer may execute the transaction at the direction of the customer. Customer suitability information specified in MSRB Rule G-19 is required to be maintained in written form.

Discretionary accounts offered to customers in municipal securities must have prior written authorization of the customer and must be accepted in writing by a municipal securities principal. All discretionary account transactions must meet suitability standards for the customer unless specifically authorized by the customer.

Churning is defined as the practice of effecting transactions that are excessive in size and frequency in view of the information known about the customer. Churning an account is prohibited.

All gifts and gratuities incidental to the bank's dealer activities are subject to MSRB Rule G-20. Generally, they are considered as gifts given in the normal course of business dealings (meals, theater tickets, etc.) limited to approximately $100 annually to any one person.

MSRB Rule G-21, "Advertising," defines advertisement as any material (other than listings of offerings) published or designed for use in the public media, or any promotional literature designed for dissemination to the public, including any notice, circular, report, market letter, form letter, or reprint or excerpt of the foregoing. The term does not apply to preliminary official statements or official statements, but does pertain to abstracts or summaries of official statements, offering circulars and other such similar documents prepared by municipal securities brokers or municipal securities dealers. The rule prohibits the bank from publishing or causing to be published any materially false or misleading advertisements concerning municipal securities or its facilities, services, or skills as a municipal securities dealer. All advertisements must be approved in writing by a municipal securities principal prior to first use, and each municipal securities dealer shall make and keep current in a separate file records of all such advertisements.

MSRB Rule G-22, "Control Relationship," concerns municipal securities transactions in which such a relationship exists. A control relationship exists when a bank controls, is controlled by, or is under common control with, the issuer of a security. For example, if a bank dealer also sat on the board of a debt-issuing school district, any transaction between the two would be subject to this rule. If such a relationship exists, the written disclosure of it must be made before completion of the transaction.

MSRB Rule G-23, "Activities of Financial Advisors," establishes ethical standards and disclosure requirements for bank dealers who act as financial advisors to issuers of municipal securities. A financial advisory relationship exists when a bank dealer renders or enters into an agreement to provide financial advisory or consultant services to an issuer for new issue municipal securities. The services are furnished by the financial advisor for a fee or other compensation (including deposits) and may include advice on the structure, timing, terms, etc., of new issue municipal securities. Conflicts of interest may exist in situations where a financial advisor also acts as underwriter in bringing a new issue to market. Rule G-23 is designed to minimize conflicts of interest when a financial advisor, also acting as underwriter, renders advice to an issuer on a new issue in such a manner as to unduly benefit the financial advisor/underwriter at the expense of the issuer. Specific rule requirements are:

- All financial advisory relationships must be evidenced by a written agreement entered into prior to, upon, or promptly after the inception of the financial advisory relationship. Such agreement must set forth the basis of compensation for services rendered.

- When a bank dealer acts as financial advisor and purchaser for the same new issue, and the issue is sold on a negotiated basis:

  - The financial advisory relationship must be terminated in writing.

  - The bank dealer must obtain express written consent from the issuer to acquire the securities on a negotiated basis.

  - At or before termination of the financial advisory relationship, the bank dealer must expressly disclose in writing to the issuer a possible conflict of interest in changing from financial advisor to purchaser as well as the source and anticipated amount of all remuneration.

  - The issuer has expressly acknowledged in writing receipt of such disclosures.

- When a bank dealer acts as a financial advisor and desires to bid on a new issue offered by the issuer on a competitive bid basis, the bank dealer must obtain the issuer's express written consent prior to submission of the bid.

- If a bank dealer acquires new issue municipal securities as outlined above, such bank dealer must disclose the existence of the financial advisory relationship to each customer who purchases the securities at or before completion of the transaction with the customer.

MSRB Rule G-24, "Use of Ownership Information Obtained in Fiduciary or Agency Capacity," prohibits the use of any nonpublic information to effect securities transactions. In that instance, a bank dealer acting in an agency capacity is forbidden to use any information obtained through this relationship without first obtaining written approval from the affected party. A prohibited data source would be the bank's trust division.

MSRB Rule G-25, "Improper Use of Assets," forbids a bank dealer from using customer funds or securities in any way that would be detrimental to the customer's best interest. Furthermore, the bank shall not guarantee any customer against loss or share in the profits or losses of municipal securities transactions.

Put options and repurchase agreements are not guarantees if their terms are provided in writing to the customer with or on the confirmation of the transaction, and records are maintained in accordance with G-8.

MSRB Rule G-26, "Customer Account Transfers," establishes procedures for transferring a customer's municipal securities account from one dealer to another. When the customer gives written notice of the transfer or municipal securities, both dealers must expedite and coordinate activities within the time frames specified in the rule.

MSRB Rule G-27, specifies, in part, that a municipal securities dealer shall supervise the activities of its associated persons and its municipal securities business. At least one municipal securities principal must be designated as responsible for:

- Enforcing the procedures specified in Rule G-27.

- Maintaining and preserving the books and records.

- Supervising the activities of municipal securities dealers of each location in which an associated person engages in municipal securities activities.

This rule also requires that the bank dealer establish, maintain, and enforce written supervisory procedures to assure compliance with all the MSRB rules and applicable provisions of securities laws, rules, and regulations. The written procedures must, at a minimum, provide for:

- The designation of at least one qualified municipal securities principal as responsible for supervision.

- The prompt review and written approval by the designated municipal securities principal of:

  - The opening of each municipal securities customer account.

  - Each transaction in municipal securities.

  - The handling of all written customer complaints.

  - All correspondence pertaining to the solicitation or execution of municipal securities.

  - Other matters required by rule to be reviewed or approved by a municipal securities principal.

- The prompt review and written approval of each municipal transaction effected for a discretionary account and the regular and frequent examination of customer accounts to detect and prevent irregularities and abuses.

MSRB Rule G-28, "Transactions with Employees and Partners of Other Municipal Securities Professionals." Any municipal securities transactions between a bank and employees or partners of other dealers require that written notice be given to the employer of such customer at the time of opening the account. This rule also requires that a duplicate copy of each transaction confirmation be sent to the customer's employer.

MSRB Rule G-29, "Availability of Board Rules." A complete, up-to-date copy of the MSRB rules must be maintained in each office of the bank where dealer activities are performed.

MSRB Rule G-30, "Prices and Commissions," requires that all principal transactions and all transactions effected in an agency capacity be done at prices and commissions that are fair and reasonable relative to the fair market value of the securities at the time of the transaction. This rule does not require that the municipal securities dealer establish written price mark-up guidelines or "as agent" fee schedules. The OCC does not think, however, that a municipal securities dealer department can be supervised adequately unless written price mark-up guidelines are established, maintained, and enforced.

MSRB Rule G-31, "Reciprocal Dealings with Municipal Securities Investment Companies," prohibits a municipal securities dealer from soliciting municipal securities transactions with or for an investment company as compensation for sales by that dealer of shares, units, or participations in that fund.

MSRB Rule G-32, "Disclosures in Connection with New Issues." In the sale of new issue securities, the bank must furnish all available information to the customer prior to sending final written confirmation. G-32 requires furnishing:

- A copy of the official statement, if received from the issuer.

- Any fees received by the bank acting as agent for the issuer.

- The underwriting spread.

- The initial offering price for each maturity in the issue.

MSRB Rule G-33, "Calculations." This rule establishes the mathematical calculations for accrued interest, interest bearing securities, and discounted securities.

MSRB Rule G-34, "CUSIP Numbers." This rule specifies that each municipal securities dealer who acquires a new issue security, either as principal or as agent, apply for and affix to the security a CUSIP number.

MSRB Rule G-35, "Arbitration." This rule provides for the establishment of an arbitration board to hear any claim, dispute, or controversy arising out of a bank's dealer activities. The arbitration committee consists of seven members appointed by the MSRB.

Underwriter Syndication

An underwriter may decide that the size of the security issue calls for a reduction of risk through the organization of a syndicate or joint account to aid in distribution and share risk exposure. Participants in an underwriting syndicate are selected on the basis of their historic participation in similar syndicates or, in the case of a new syndicate or participant, on their ability to sell their share of the overall commitment. Banks managing a syndicate usually fund the transaction until participants can arrange the issue's distribution. It is important that syndicate members have sufficient financial resources to purchase undistributed bonds that remain when the syndicate account is terminated.

A written syndicate agreement or letter binds the members to specific terms. That agreement specifies or provides a means of determining:

- The liability of each participant.

- The amount of good faith deposit required.

- Offering terms.

- Price concessions to members.

- Bond and expense allocations.

- The account's termination date.

- The discretionary rights of the syndicate manager.

Syndicates that underwrite serial maturity bonds occasionally operate as undivided accounts with the syndicate manager allocating groups of maturities to encourage large block sales. Such undivided liability means that account members are jointly liable for their proportionate share of all unsold bonds, regardless of their individual sales. In underwriting single maturity term issues, divided selling accounts generally are used, whereby each participant is only liable for the disposition of its proportionate share of the issue.

Underwriter inventories normally sell quickly, and the success of a large offering can be measured by the percentage of the issue that sells in the initial stage of a public offering. Smaller issues often move more slowly, but all offerings should generally sell within 30 days. Extended term underwriter inventories are usually the product of adverse market conditions or inaccurate pricing.

An area of potential legal liability and conflict of interest exists in the purchase, by a bank's trading or permanent portfolio departments, of securities underwritten by the bank. There may be a legitimate reason for such a purchase; for example, it may be considered an attractive investment by permanent portfolio supervisors. However, under certain circumstances, such acquisition may actually constitute impermissible "withholding" or "dumping."

"Withholding" is when an underwriter retains an attractive issue for its own or associated accounts without making a bona fide public offering. When a bank withholds part of an issue and market demand exceeds the available supply, withholding can artificially raise the price. That may become apparent when the initial offering price is subject to significant increases because of sales activity initiated by the underwriter bank acting as principal or as agent for associated parties, i.e., employees and directors or their interests, affiliates, and trust accounts.

"Dumping" is when a bank attempts to defer losses on an unsuccessful offering by transferring the securities to the bank's trading inventory or permanent portfolio at original cost. Such transfers are only acceptable when the marketability, quality, and maturity of the securities are consistent with pre-established trading and investment policy guidelines and at an independently established market price as of the date of transfer. If an independent market price cannot be established, carrying values should be based on the last "arm's length" bid or on values determined by comparative yield pricing analysis.

In order to avoid potential conflicts of interest, policy should define acceptable relationships between the underwriting section and investment portfolio areas.

Secondary Market Trading

Trading in municipal securities takes place in an over-the-counter secondary market. Municipal securities dealers do not make formal markets in their securities, offering prices are quoted, and bids are seldom made public. Prices for most general obligation bonds are quoted on a yield-to-maturity basis, which can be converted to a dollar price by using a "basis book." Daily offering prices of more actively traded bonds are published in "The Blue List of Current Municipal Offerings" or shown through wire services. Prices for municipal security secondary market trades are negotiated.

The market risk inherent in secondary market trading results from the impact of market price changes on trading inventories. In order to reduce their vulnerability to market risk, bank dealers must practice some form of inventory management.

Inventories that include long-term holdings of high yield, lower quality bonds and that appear large relative to sales volume, are characteristic of bank dealers that assume high market risks. Such holdings can generate substantial trading profits in a favorable market, and in a mildly adverse market, they can be held for their yield. However, in a declining market, the bank is exposed to substantial principal losses.

Disciplined traders avoid the temptation to hold securities for extended periods in anticipation of large profits. They minimize market risk by carefully positioning securities that sell profitably and quickly. That is accomplished by having quality and maturity features compatible with customer needs. Bonds that do not move quickly are subject to price mark-downs and are disposed of through inter-dealer trading. A rapid turnover of bonds at moderate profits usually produces steady income and limits market risks.

Banks sometimes maintain very small inventory positions, preferring to conduct the bulk of their business in "riskless" transactions. They function as intermediaries for other municipal securities dealers by taking temporary options to sell securities owned by the other dealers. The securities are "shown" or offered by another dealer, and the bank takes a no obligation option to buy them at a certain price less a modest dealer concession and attempts to resell them at the original offering price. Thus, the bank dealer earns a moderate income, is consistently making new offerings, and keeps its sales force productively occupied without assuming any market risk.

Inventory Management

Inventory management guidelines are a vital part of any municipal securities trading policy. Procedures should be established limiting the total inventory of securities as well as positions in securities of a single or related obligors. Commitments to buy securities should be included in such limits. Acceptable quality and maturity characteristics should be defined, and limits should be prescribed for securities with common maturities and no, or low, ratings. The length of time a security may be inventoried, the way it will be evaluated if held for an extended term, and stop-loss sales provisions should be described. Individual responsibilities for executing various size trades and for reviewing trades and inventory positions should be fixed. The dealers with which the bank will transact business should be selected based on defined professional standards of competence, financial strength, and integrity.

Reporting and Operations

Reporting

Securities held for trading purposes and the income and expense that results from trading activities should be isolated by specific general ledger or journal accounts. The balances in those accounts should be included in the appropriate reporting captions on the report of condition and the report of income.

Due bills that are issued to obtain funds for general banking purposes should be reported as "liabilities for borrowed monies" on the report of condition. Those due bills are, however, subject to the restrictions imposed by regulations D and Q.

Short-sales of securities borrowed should not be deducted from securities inventory positions. Other asset and other liability accounts should be established to reflect the value of, and liability for, the borrowed securities used to complete the short-sale transaction. Short-sales of like securities that are held in the bank's investment portfolio should be recorded as regular sales, unless pledge or repurchase encumbrances require the bank to borrow a security to complete delivery.

12 CFR 11 and 18 require banks to report the carrying value of trading inventories on the same basis as used for tax purposes. The acceptable procedures for valuing trading inventories for tax purposes include valuation at cost or market, or the lower of cost or market. Prudent banking practice and generally accepted accounting principles require securities trading inventories to be reported at market value. Accordingly, the carrying values of trading security inventories should be revalued monthly to reflect current market prices. The increase or decrease in unrealized appreciation or depreciation

resulting from that revaluation should be credited or charged to income. Periodic independent revaluation is the most effective means of measuring the trading decisions of bank management.

For reporting purposes the trading department's income should include, not only revaluation adjustments, but also coupon interest, profits and losses from the sale of securities, and other items related to the purchase and sale of trading securities. Salaries, commissions, and other expenses should be excluded.

Operations

A bank dealer's operational functions should be designed to regulate the custody and movement of securities and to adequately account for trading transactions. Because of the dollar volume and speed of trading activities, operational inefficiencies can quickly result in major problems.

In some cases, a bank may not receive or deliver a security by settlement date. When a bank fails to receive a security by the settlement date, a liability exists until the transaction is consummated or canceled. When the security is not delivered to the contra-party by settlement date, a receivable exists until that "fail" is resolved. "Fails" to deliver for an extended time or a substantial number of cancellations are sometimes characteristic of poor operational control or questionable trading activities. Fails should be controlled by prompt reporting and follow-up procedures. The use of multi-copy confirmation forms enables operational personnel to retain and file a copy by settlement date and should allow for prompt fail reporting and resolution.

Security borrowing or lending is frequently used to facilitate trading operations. That type of transaction requires the pledging of similar quality securities as collateral. Collateral margins vary with the maturity of the pledged security. Shorter maturities generally require smaller margins and longer maturities, wider coverage. The minimum recommended margin is 102 percent market value collateral coverage. Collateral should be compared to the market values frequently if adequate coverage is to be maintained. Policy standards regarding approved borrowers, acceptable collateral, adequate collateral margins, and revaluation procedures should be established, and compliance with policy standards should be controlled by designating an officer to review, approve, and initial each transaction. See BC196.

Policy Summary

The legal responsibilities of the bank's directors require that they insure that bank dealer activities are conducted on a sound and legal basis. That only can be accomplished if the directors endorse a written trading policy that addresses each area of market and legal risk. Compliance with policy can be monitored by reporting and reviewing systems that require a positive response from a qualified bank officer before a trading transaction can be executed. Written policy guidelines should be distributed to each individual engaged in trading activities.

1. Review compliance examination results for Municipal Securities Rulemaking Board rules or Government Securities Act. If compliance examination is being conducted concurrently, coordinate with examiner(s) assigned responsibility for MSRB or GSA to avoid duplication.

2. Complete or update the Bank Dealer Activities section of Internal Control Questionnaire.

3. Based on the evaluation of internal controls and the work performed by internal/external auditors (see separate work program), determine the scope of the examination.

4. Test for compliance with policies, practices, procedures, and internal controls in conjunction with performing the remaining examination procedures. Also, obtain a listing of any deficiencies noted in the latest review done by internal/external auditors from the examiner assigned "Internal and External Audits," and determine if corrections have been accomplished.

5. Perform appropriate verification procedures.

6. Request that the bank prepare the following schedules. Coordinate with compliance examiner to avoid duplication.

    a. An aged schedule of securities that have been acquired as a result of underwriting activities.

    b. An aged schedule of trading account securities and money market instruments held for trading or arbitrage purposes. Reflect commitments to purchase and sell securities and all joint account interests.

    c. A schedule of short-sale transactions.

    d. An aged schedule of due bills.

e. A list of bonds borrowed.

f. An aged schedule of "fails" to receive or deliver securities on unsettled contracts.

g. A schedule of approved securities borrowers and approved limits.

h. A schedule of loaned securities.

i. A schedule detailing account names and/or account numbers of the following customer accounts:

- Own bank trust accounts.
- Own bank permanent portfolio account.
- Affiliated banks' permanent portfolio accounts.
- Personal accounts of bank employees.
- Personal accounts of employees of other banks.
- Accounts of brokers or other dealers.
- Personal accounts of employees of other brokers or dealers.
- Accounts opened within the past 3 months.

j. A list of all joint accounts entered into since the last examination.

k. A list of all underwritings since the last examination and whether such securities were acquired by negotiation or competitive bid.

l. A list of all financial advisory relationships.

m. A sales production report or similar report detailing the sales performance of persons engaged in securities sales.

n. A listing of all bonuses, sales credits, and compensation (current and/or deferred) for all securities professionals employed.

7. Agree balances of appropriate schedules to general ledger, and review reconciling items for reasonableness.

8. Determine the extent and effectiveness of trading policy supervision by:

a. Reviewing the abstracted minutes of the board of directors meetings and/or of any appropriate committee.

b. Determining that proper authorization for the trading officer or committee has been made.

c. Ascertaining the limitations or restrictions on delegated authorities.

d. Evaluating the sufficiency of analytical data used in the most recent board or committee trading department review.

e. Reviewing the methods of reporting by department supervisors and internal auditors to insure compliance with established policy and law. Coordinate with compliance examiner.

f. Reaching a conclusion about the effectiveness of director supervision of the bank's trading policy. Prepare a memo for the examiner assigned "Duties and Responsibilities of Directors" stating your conclusions. All conclusions should be supported by factual documentation.

(Before continuing, refer to steps 15 and 16. They should be performed in conjunction with the remaining examination steps.)

9.   Ascertain the general character of underwriting activities and the effectiveness of department management by reviewing underwriter files and ledgers, committee reports and offering statements to determine:

a. The significance of underwriting activities and direct placements of Type III securities as reflected by the volume of sales and profit or loss on operations. Compare current data to comparable prior periods.

b. Whether there is a recognizable pattern in:

- The extent of analysis of material information relating to the ability of the issuer to service the obligation.
- Rated quality of offerings.
- Point spread or profit margin for unrated issues.

- Geographic distribution of issuers.
- Syndicate participants.
- Bank's trust department serving as corporate trustee, paying agent and transfer agent for issuers.
- Trustee, paying agent, and transfer agent business being placed with institutions that purchase a significant percentage of the underwriter or private placement offering.

    c. The volume of outstanding bids. Compare current data to comparable prior periods.

    d. The maturity, rated quality, and geographic distribution of takedowns from syndicate participations.

    e. The extent of transfer to the bank's own or affiliated investment or trading portfolios or to trust accounts.

10. Determine the general character of trading account activities and whether the activities are in conformance with stated policy, by:

    a. Reviewing departmental reports, budgets, and position records for various categories of trading activity and determining:

- The significance of present sales volume compared to comparable prior periods and departmental budgets.
- Whether the bank's objectives are compatible with the volume of trading activity.

    b. Reviewing customer lists and approved dealer lists and/or joint account participants to determine:

- Character of market penetration.
- The nature of customer business activities.
- Geographic distribution of customers.

11. Review customer ledgers, securities position ledgers, transaction, or purchase and sales journals, and analyze the soundness of the bank's trading practices by:

a. Reviewing a representative sample of agency and contemporaneous principal trades and determining the commission and price mark-up parameters for various sizes and types of transactions.

b. Selecting principal transactions that have resulted in large profits and determining if the transaction involved:

   - "Buy-backs" of previously traded securities.
   - Own bank or affiliated bank portfolios.
   - A security that has unusual quality and maturity characteristics.

c. Reviewing significant inventory positions taken since the prior examination and determining if:

   - The quality and maturity of the inventory position was compatible with prudent banking practices.
   - The size of the position was within prescribed limits and compatible with a sound trading strategy.

d. Determining the bank's exposure on repurchase transactions by:

   - Reviewing the maturities of "repo" and "reverse repo" agreements to ascertain the existence, duration, amounts, and strategy used to manage unmatched maturity "gaps" and extended (over 30 days) maturities.
   - Reviewing records since the last examination to determine the aggregate amounts of:
     - Matched repurchase transactions.
     - "Reverse repo" financing extended to one or related firm(s).
     - "Repo" source funds obtained from a single or related customer(s).
   - Performing credit analysis of significant concentrations with any single or related entity(ies).
   - Reporting the relationship of those concentrations to the examiners assigned "Concentrations of Credit" and "Funds Management."

12. Determine the extent of risk inherent in trading account securities which have been in inventory in excess of 30 days and:

a. Determine the dollar volume in extended holdings.

b. Determine the amounts of identifiable positions with regard to issue, issuer, yield, credit rating, and maturity.

c. Determine the current market value for individual issues that show an internal valuation mark-down of 10 percent or more.

d. Perform credit analyses on the issuers of nonrated holdings identified as significant positions.

e. Perform credit analyses on those issues with valuation write-downs considered significant relative to the scope of trading operations.

f. Discuss plans for disposal of slow moving inventories with management, and determine the reasonableness of those plans in light of current and projected market trends.

13. Using an appropriate sampling technique, select issues from the schedule of trading account inventory. If verification procedures have been performed, use the same sample. Test valuation procedures by:

a. Reviewing operating procedures and supporting work papers and determining if prescribed valuation procedures are being followed.

b. Comparing bank prepared market prices, as of the most recent valuation date, to an independent pricing source (use trade date "bid" prices).

c. Investigating any price differences noted.

14. Using an appropriate sampling technique, select transactions from the schedule of short-sales and determine:

a. The degree of speculation reflected by basis point spreads.

b. Present exposure shown by computing the cost to cover short-sales.

c. If transactions are reversed in a reasonable period of time.

d. If the bank makes significant use of due bill transactions to obtain funds for its banking business:

- Coordinate with the examiner assigned "Review of Regulatory Reports" to determine if the bank's reports of condition reflect due bill transactions as "liabilities for borrowed money."
- Report amounts, duration, seasonal patterns, and budgeted projections for due bills to the examiner assigned "Funds Management."

15. Analyze the effectiveness of operational controls by reviewing recent cancellations and fail items that are a week or more beyond settlement date and determine:

a. The amount of extended fails.

b. The planned disposition of extended fails.

c. If the control system allows a timely, productive follow-up on unresolved fails.

d. The reasons for cancellations.

e. The planned disposition of securities that have been inventoried prior to the recognition of a fail or a cancellation.

16. Coordinate with examiner responsible for compliance examination, and determine compliance with applicable laws, rulings, and regulations by performing the following for:

a. 12 CFR 1.3 — Eligible Securities:

- Review inventory schedules of underwriting and trading accounts, and determine if issues whose par value is in excess of 10 percent of the bank's capital and unimpaired surplus are Type I securities.
- Determine that the total par value of Type II investments does not exceed 10 percent of the bank's capital and unimpaired surplus, based on the combination of holdings and permanent portfolio positions in the same securities.

- Elicit management's comments and review underwriting records on direct placement of Type III securities for its own account by ascertaining if direct placement issues have been placed in own bank or affiliated investment portfolios, or if underwriting proceeds were used to reduce affiliate loans.

b. 12 CFR 18 — Shareholders and 12 CFR 11 — Securities Exchange Act Disclosure Rules:

If the bank operates a trading account, review the bank's reports filed pursuant to these rules and determine that trading assets and net trading income are reported separately.

c. 12 USC 371(c) and 375 — Preferential Treatment:

Obtain a list of domestic affiliate relationships and a list of directors and principal officers and their business interests from appropriate examiners, and determine whether transactions, include securities clearance services, involving affiliates, insiders or their interests are on terms less favorable to the bank than those transactions involving unrelated parties.

d. 12 CFR 9.12 — Purchase of Securities Involving Fiduciary Funds:

Review customer ledgers, and determine if trading or underwriting securities were purchased with funds held by the bank in a fiduciary capacity.

e. 12 CFR 204.2 and BC-182 — Due Bills:

- Review outstanding due bills, and determine if:
    - The customer was provided full written disclosure of all material facts and circumstances concerning each due bill.
    - Safekeeping receipts are sent to safekeeping customers only after the purchased security has been delivered.
- Review bank practices for due bills, and determine if they are issued only in those situations where the bank, despite a diligent good faith effort, is unable to deliver the securities purchased by the customer at settlement.

- If such a good faith effort is not evident, determine that demand deposit reserves are maintained from the date of receipt of customer funds, and that the customer is informed of the bank's intentions with respect to obtaining securities sold.
- Review due bills outstanding over three business days, and determine if they are collateralized or properly reserved.
- Review collateralized due bills, and determine if the liability is secured by securities of the same type and of comparable maturity and with a market value at least equal to that of the security that is the subject of the due bill.
- If the bank has accepted customer funds for purchase of U.S. government securities, but has not placed the order by the close of the next business day after receipt, has the bank immediately deposited or redeposited funds in the customer's account, and has the bank sent the customer notice of such deposit, or has the bank complied with the "buy-in" provisions of the GSA?

f. 12 USC 84 — Borrowed and Loaned Securities:

Review lists of borrowed and loaned securities, and determine if the collateral pledged is composed of securities similar to and with a market value at least equal to that of the borrowed or loaned securities. Apply the limits of 12 USC 84 to lending arrangements.

g. 12 CFR 217.4(d) — Purchase of Own Bank Time Deposit Prior to Maturity.

Review negotiable CD inventory position ledgers and determine if the bank has acquired its own CDs.

h. 17 CFR 240.17f-1 — Lost and Stolen Securities Program:

Consult with the examiner assigned the review of regulatory reports to determine if the bank is registered with the Securities Information Center, Inc. as a direct or indirect inquirer for the lost and stolen securities program. Determine the adequacy of the bank's compliance with the lost and stolen securities program.

17. Coordinate with examiner assigned responsibility for compliance examination or review the results of previous compliance examination.

Test for unsafe and unsound practices and possible violations of 15 USC 78j by:

a. Reviewing customer account schedules of own bank and affiliated bank permanent portfolios, trusts, other broker/dealers, employees of own or other banks and other broker/dealers. Use an appropriate sampling technique to select transactions, and compare trade prices to independently established market prices as of the date of trade.

b. Reviewing transactions, including U.S government tender offer subscription files, involving employees and directors of own or other banks and determine if the funds used in the transactions were misused bank funds or the proceeds of reciprocal or preferential loans.

c. Reviewing sales to affiliated companies to determine that the sold securities were not subsequently repurchased at an additional markup and that gains were not recognized a second time.

d. Reviewing commercial paper sales journals or confirmations to determine whether the bank sells affiliate commercial paper. If so, determine whether:

  • The bank engages in affiliate-issued commercial paper only "as agent" and only with sophisticated investors.
  • Transactions are generally denominated in amounts of $25,000 or more.
  • Each transaction confirmation clearly discloses that the affiliate-issued commercial paper is not a deposit and is not insured by the FDIC.

e. Reviewing securities position records and customer ledgers with respect to large volume repetitive purchase and sales transactions and:

  • Independently testing market prices of significant transactions that involve the purchase and resale of the same security to the same or related parties.
  • Investigating the purchase of large blocks of securities from dealer

firms just prior to month end and their subsequent resale to the same firm just after the beginning of the next month.

f. Selecting a representative sample of customer accounts opened during the last 3 months and determining:

- The percentage of the total number of selected accounts that involve customers located outside of the bank's service area.
- The manner in which the new customers' names were selected for solicitation.
- The extent of information in the file concerning inquiry into the customers' financial condition and investment needs.
- If initial trades for new customers were executed at market price by comparing trade prices to independently established market prices.

g. Reviewing lists of approved dealer firms and determining that the approval of any firm that handles a significant volume of agency transactions is based on competitive factors rather than deposit relationships.

h. Reviewing customer complaint files and determining the reasons for such complaints.

18. Consult with the examiner assigned to dealer compliance review, or review the results of the prior compliance examination. Assess the dealer department's overall compliance effort by reviewing the responses to the MSRB and GSA compliance procedures.

19. Discuss with an appropriate officer and prepare report comments concerning:

a. The soundness of trading objectives, policies, and practices.

b. The degree of legal and market risk assumed by trading operations.

c. The effectiveness of analytical, reporting, and control systems.

d. Violations of law.

e. Internal control deficiencies.

f. Apparent or potential conflicts of interest.

g. Other matters of significance.

20. Reach a conclusion regarding the quality of department management, and state your conclusions on the management brief provided by the examiner assigned "Management Appraisal."

21. Prepare a memorandum, and update work programs with any information that will facilitate future examinations.

Review the bank's internal controls, policies, practices, and procedures regarding bank dealer activities. The bank's system should be documented in a complete, concise manner and should include, where appropriate, narrative descriptions, flowcharts, copies of forms used, and other pertinent information. Items marked with asterisks require substantiation by observation or testing. Check marks at the end of lines indicate information not specifically required by MSRB rule G-8.

Securities Underwriting Trading Policies

1. Has the board of directors, consistent with its duties and responsibilities, adopted written securities underwriting/trading policies that:

    a. Outline objectives?

    b. Establish limits and/or guidelines for:

    - Price mark-ups?
    - Quality of issues?
    - Maturity of issues?
    - Inventory positions (including WI positions)?
    - Amounts of unrealized loss on inventory positions?
    - Length of time an issue will be carried in inventory?
    - Amounts of individual trades or underwriter interests?
    - Acceptability of brokers and syndicate partners?

    c. Recognize possible conflicts of interest and establish appropriate procedures regarding:

    - Deposit and service relationships with municipalities whose issues have underwriting links to the trading department?
    - Deposit relationships with securities firms handling significant volumes of agency transactions or syndicate participations?
    - Transfers made between trading account inventory and investment portfolio(s)?

- The bank's trust department acting as trustee, paying agent, and transfer agent for issues which have an underwriting relationship with the trading department?

d. State procedures for periodic or monthly valuation of trading inventories to market value or to the lower of cost or market price?

e. State procedures for periodic independent verification of valuations of the trading inventories?

f. Outline methods of internal review and reporting by department supervisors, compliance managers, and internal auditors to insure compliance with established policy?

g. Identify permissible types of securities?

h. Ensure compliance with the rules of fair practice that:

- Prohibit any deceptive, dishonest, or unfair practice?
- Adopt formal suitability checklists?
- Monitor gifts and gratuities?
- Prohibit materially false or misleading advertisements?
- Provide for the disclosures and consents necessary to avoid conflicts of interest when the bank assumes the role of both underwriter and financial advisor to the issuer?
- Adopt a system to determine the existence of possible control relationships?
- Prohibit the use of confidential, nonpublic information without written approval of the affected parties?
- Prohibit improper use of funds held on another's behalf?
- Designate specific principals to supervise personnel and business conduct in general?
- Adopt written securities price mark-up guidelines?
- Allocate responsibility for transactions with own employees and employees of other dealers?
- Require the maintenance of the MSRB manual at each office where there are representatives?
- Require disclosure on all new issues?

i.   Provide for exceptions to standard policy?

2.   Are the underwriting/trading policies reviewed at least quarterly by the board to determine their adequacy in light of changing conditions?

3.   Is there a periodic review by the board to assure that the underwriting/trading department is in compliance with its policies?

Supervisory Procedures

4.   Does the municipal securities dealer provide adequate supervision for its activities by:

   a.   Designating an appropriately qualified individual(s) to:

   - Supervise the activities of the municipal securities dealer and enforce the required written procedures? If so, give name.
   - Maintain and preserve the books and records required by rules G-8 and G-9? If so, give name.

   b.   Establishing written supervisory procedures that:

   - Designate one or more municipal securities principals to supervise the activities of the dealer?
   - Provide for prompt review and written approval by the designated municipal securities principal of:
   - The opening of each customer account carried by the bank?
   - Each transaction in municipal securities?
   - All written customer complaints pertaining to transactions in municipal securities?
   - All correspondence pertinent to the solicitation or execution of transactions in municipal securities?

   c.   Providing for the prompt review and written approval of each transaction in municipal securities effected with or for a discretionary account introduced or carried?

   d.   Providing for the regular and frequent examination by the designated municipal securities principal of customer accounts introduced or carried to detect and prevent irregularities and abuses?

5. Does the bank have accounts for anyone employed by, or partner of, another municipal securities dealer or on the behalf of any spouse or minor child of such person? If so:

    *   Has written notice of the opening and maintenance of such account been given first to the broker or dealer by whom such person is employed?
    *   Has the bank sent a confirmation notice to the employing dealer simultaneous with the notice sent to the customer at the time of effecting a transaction?
    *   Has the bank acted according to any written instructions that may have been provided by the employing dealer or broker?

6. Does the bank maintain a complete, updated copy of all MSRB rules in each office in which any municipal security dealer activities are conducted?

7. When the bank sold new issue municipal securities to customers, determine if:

    *   A copy of the official statement furnished on behalf of the issuer was sent to the customer?
    *   In the instance of a negotiated sale of a new issue, was the following information sent to the customer:
        *   The underwriting spread?
        *   The amount of any fee received by the municipal securities dealer as agent for the issuer in the distribution of the securities?
        *   The initial offering price for each maturity in the issue that is offered or to be offered in whole or in part by the underwriters?

    Those requirements must be met at or prior to the sending of the final confirmation notice.

8. Has the bank advertised any new issues of securities, or part thereof, showing the initial reoffering prices or yields for the securities, even if the price or yield for a maturity or maturities may have changed? If so:

- Did the advertisements contain the date of sale of the securities by the issuer to the syndicate?
- Did the advertisement show either the initial reoffering prices or yields or the prices or yields that existed at the time the advertisement was placed for publication?

9. Has the bank advertised any municipal securities or municipal securities services through public media or other promotional material designed for customers? If so:

- Are advertisements reviewed to determine they are not false or misleading?
- Are advertisements approved by a principal prior to "first use"?

Offsetting Resale and Repurchase Transactions

10. Has the board of directors, consistent with its duties and responsibilities, adopted written offsetting repurchase transaction policies that:

a. Limit the aggregate amount of repurchase transactions?

b. Limit the amounts in unmatched or extended (over 30 days) maturity transactions?

c. Determine maximum time gaps for unmatched maturity transactions?

d. Determine minimally acceptable interest rate spreads for various maturity transactions?

e. Determine the maximum amount of funds to be extended to any single or related firms through "reverse repo" transactions, involving unsold (through forward sales) securities?

f. Require firms involved in "reverse repo" transactions to submit corporate resolutions stating the names and limits of individuals, who are authorized to commit the firm?

g. Require submission of current financial information by firms involved in "reverse repo" transactions?

h. Provide for periodic credit reviews and approvals for firms involved in "reverse repo" transactions?

i. Specify types of acceptable repurchase transaction collateral (if so, indicate type _____).

11. Are written collateral control procedures designed so that:

a. Collateral assignment forms are used?

b. Collateral assignments of registered securities are accompanied by powers of attorney signed by the registered owner?

- Registered securities are registered in bank or bank's nominee name when they are assigned as collateral for extended maturity (over 30 days) "reverse repo" transactions?

c. Funds are not disbursed until "reverse repo" collateral is delivered into the physical custody of the bank or an independent safekeeping agent?

d. Funds are only advanced against predetermined collateral margins or discounts?

- If so, indicate margin or discount percentage _____.

e. Collateral margins or discounts are predicted upon:

- The type of security pledged as collateral?
- Maturity of collateral?
- Historic and anticipated price volatility of the collateral?
- Maturity of the "reverse repo" agreements?

f. Maintenance agreements are required to support pre-determined collateral margin or discount?

g. Maintenance agreements are structured to allow margin calls in the event of collateral price declines?

h. Collateral market value is frequently checked to determine compliance with margin and maintenance requirements (if so, indicate frequency _____)?

Custody and Movement of Securities

12. *Are the bank's procedures such that persons do not have sole custody of securities in that:

a. They do not have sole physical access to securities?

b. They do not prepare disposal documents that are not also approved by authorized persons?

c. For the security custodian, supporting disposal documents are examined or adequately tested by a second custodian?

d. No person authorizes more than one of the following transactions: execution of trades, receipt and delivery of securities, and collection or disbursement of payment?

13. *Are securities physically safeguarded to prevent loss, unauthorized disposal, or use? And:

a. Are negotiable securities kept under dual control?

b. Are securities counted frequently, on a surprise basis, reconciled to the securities record, and the results of such counts reported to management?

c. Does the bank periodically test for compliance with provisions of its insurance policies regarding custody of securities?

d. For securities in the custody of others:

- Are custody statements agreed periodically to position ledgers, and any differences followed up to a conclusion?
- Are statements received from brokers and other dealers reconciled promptly, and any differences followed up to a conclusion?

- Are positions for which no statements are received confirmed periodically, and stale items followed up to a conclusion?

14. Are trading account securities segregated from other bank owned securities or securities held in safekeeping for customers?

15. *Is access to the trading securities vault restricted to authorized employees?

16. Do withdrawal authorizations require countersignatures to indicate security count verifications?

17. Is registered mail used for mailing securities, and are adequate receipt files maintained for such mailings (if registered mail is used for some but not all mailings, indicate criteria and reasons)?

18. Are pre-numbered forms used to control securities trades, movements and payments?

19. If so, is numerical control of pre-numbered forms accounted for periodically by persons independent of those activities?

20. Do alterations to forms governing the trade, movement, and payment of securities require:

   a. *Signature of the authorizing party?

   b. Use of a change of instruction form?

21. With respect to negotiability of registered securities:

   a. Are securities kept in non-negotiable form whenever possible?

   b. Are all securities received, and not immediately delivered, transferred to the name of the bank or its nominee and kept in non-negotiable form whenever possible?

   c. Are securities received checked for negotiability (endorsements, signature, guarantee, legal opinion, etc.) and for completeness (coupons, warrants, etc.) before they are placed in the vault?

Records Maintenance

22.   Does the bank maintain:

   a.   Order tickets which include:

   - Capacity as principal or agent?
   - If order is firm or conditional?
   - Terms, conditions, or instructions and modifications?
   - Type of transaction (purchase or sale)?
   - Execution price?
   - Description of security?
   - Date and time of order receipt?
   - Date and time of execution?
   - Dealer's or customer's name?
   - Delivery and payment instructions?
   - Terms, conditions, date and time of cancellation of an agency order?

   b.   Customer confirmations, including as applicable (required by MSRB Rule G-15):

   - Bank dealer's name, address, and phone number?
   - Customer's name?
   - Designation of whether transaction was a purchase from or sale to the customer?
   - Par value of securities?
   - Description of securities, including at a minimum:
     - Name of issuer?
     - Interest rate?
     - Maturity rate?
     - Designation, if securities are limited tax?
     - Subject to redemption prior to maturity (callable)?
     - Designation, if revenue bonds and the type of revenue?
     - The name of any company or person in addition to the issuer who is obligated, directly or indirectly, to pay debt service on revenue bonds? (In the case of more than one such obligor, the

phrase "multiple obligors" will suffice.)
- Dated date, if it affects price or interest calculations?
- First interest payment date, if other than semi-annual?
- Designation, if securities are "fully registered" or "registered as principal"?
- Designation, if securities are "pre-refunded"?
- Designation, if securities have been "called," maturity date fixed by call notice and amount of call price?
- Denominations of bearer bonds, if other than denominations of $1,000 and $5,000 par value?
- Denominations of registered bonds, if other than multiples of $1,000 par value up to $100,000 par value?
- Denominations of municipal notes?
- CUSIP number, if assigned?
- Trade date and time of execution, or a statement that time of execution will be furnished upon written request of the customer?
- Settlement date?
- Yield and dollar price? Only the dollar price need be shown for securities traded at par.
  - For transactions in callable securities effected on a yield basis, the resulting price calculated to the lowest of price to call premium, par option (callable at par) or to maturity, and if priced to premium call or par option, a statement to that effect and the call or option date and price used in the calculation?
  - For transactions in callable securities effected on the basis of dollar price, the resulting yield calculated to lowest of yield to premium call, par option or maturity?
- Amount of accrued interest?
- Extended principal amount?
- Total dollar amount of transaction?
- The capacity in which the bank dealer effected the transaction:
  - As principal for own account?
  - As agent for customer?
  - As agent for a person other than the customer?
  - As agent for both the customer and another person (dual agent)?
- If a transaction is effected as agent for the customer or as dual agent:
  - Either the name of the contra-party or a statement that the

information will be furnished upon request?
- The source and amount of any commission or other remuneration to the bank dealer?
- Payment and delivery instructions?
- Special instructions, such as:
  - "Ex-legal" (traded without legal opinion)?
  - "Flat" (traded without interest)?
  - "In default" as to principal or interest?

c. Dealer confirmations, including as applicable (required by MSRB Rule G-12):

- Bank dealer's name, address and telephone number?
- Contra-party identification?
- Designation of purchase from or sale to?
- Par value of securities?
- Description of securities, including at a minimum:
  - Name of issuer?
  - Interest rate?
  - Maturity date?
  - Designation, if securities are limited tax?
  - Subject to redemption prior to maturity (callable)?
  - Designation, if revenue bonds and the type of revenue?
  - The name of any company or person in addition to the issuer who is obligated, directly or indirectly, to pay debt service on revenue bonds? (In the case of more than one such obligor, the phrase "multiple obligors" will suffice.)
  - Dated date, if it affects price or interest calculations?
  - First interest payment date, if other than semi-annual?
  - Designation, if securities are "fully registered" or "registered as principal"?
  - Designation, if securities are "pre-refunded"?
  - Designation, if securities have been "called," maturity date fixed by call notice and amount of call price?
  - Denominations of bearer bonds, if other than denominations of $1,000 and $5,000 par value?
  - Denominations of registered bonds, if other than multiples of $1,000 par value up to $100,000 par value?
  - Denominations of municipal notes?
- CUSIP number, if assigned?

- Trade date?
- Settlement date?
- Yield to maturity and resulting dollar price? Only the dollar price need be shown for securities traded at par or on a dollar basis.
  - For transactions in callable securities effected on a yield basis, the resulting price calculated to the lowest of price to call premium, par option (callable at par) or to maturity?
  - If applicable, the fact that securities are priced to premium call or par option and the call or option date and price used in the calculation?
- Amount of accrued interest?
- Extended principal amount?
- Total dollar amount of transaction?
- Payment and delivery instructions?
- Special instructions, such as:
  - "Ex-legal" (traded without legal opinion)?
  - "Flat" (traded without interest)?
  - "In default" as to principal or interest?

d. Purchase and sale journals or blotters which include:

- Trade date?
- Description of securities?
- Aggregate par value?
- Unit dollar price or yield?
- Aggregate trade price?
- Accrued interest?
- Name of buyer or seller?
- Name of party received from or delivered to?
- Bond or note numbers?
- Indication if securities are in registered form?
- Receipts or disbursements of cash?
- Specific designation of "when issued" transactions?
- Transaction or confirmation numbers recorded in consecutive sequence to insure that transactions are not omitted? ✓
- Other references to documents of original entry? ✓

e. Short-sale ledgers which include:

- Sale price? ✓
- Settlement date?
- Present market value? ✓
- Basis point spread? ✓
- Description of collateral? ✓
- Cost of collateral or cost to acquire collateral? ✓
- Carrying charges? ✓

f. Security position ledgers showing separately for each security positioned for the bank's own account:

- Description of the security?
- Posting date (either trade or settlement date, provided posting date is consistent with other records of original entry)?
- Aggregate par value?
- Cost?
- Average cost? ✓
- Location?
- Count differences classified by the date on which they were discovered?
  (For questions dealing with position ledgers, multiple maturities of the same issue of municipal securities and multiple coupons of the same maturity may be shown on the same record, provided that adequate secondary records separately identify such maturities and coupons.)

g. Securities transfer or validation ledgers which include:

- Address where securities were sent?
- Date sent?
- Description of security?
- Aggregate par value?
- If registered securities:
  - Present name of record?
  - New name to be registered?
- Old certificate or note numbers?
- New certificate or note numbers?
- Date returned?

h. Securities received and delivered journals or tickets which include:

- Date of receipt or delivery?
- Name of sender and receiver?
- Description of security?
- Aggregate par value?
- Trade and settlement dates?
- Certificate numbers?

i. Cash or wire transfer receipt and disbursement tickets which include:

- Draft or check numbers?
- Customer accounts debited or credited?
- Notation of the original entry item that initiated the transaction?

j. Cash or wire transfer journals which additionally include:

- Draft or check reconcilement?
- Daily totals of cash debits and credits?
- Daily proofs?

k. Fail ledgers which include:

- Description of security?
- Aggregate par value?
- Price?
- Fail date? ✓
- Date included on fail ledger? ✓
- Customer or dealer name?
- Resolution date?
- A distinction between a customer and a dealer fail?
- Follow-up detail regarding efforts to resolve the fail? ✓

l. Due bill ledgers which include:

- Description of securities sold?
- Aggregate par value?

- Price?
- Date of receipt of customer funds?
- Customer name?
- Description of collateral?
- Market value of collateral?
- Date collateral was assigned or deposit reserve treatment commenced?
- Date securities sold were delivered?

m. Securities borrowed and loaned ledgers which include:

- Date of transaction?
- Description of securities?
- Aggregate par value?
- Market value of securities? ✓
- Contra-party name?
- Value at which security was loaned?
- Date returned?
- Description of collateral? ✓
- Aggregate par value of collateral? ✓
- Market value of collateral? ✓
- Collateral safekeeping location? ✓
- Dates of periodic valuations? ✓

n. Records concerning written or oral put options, guarantee and repurchase agreements which include:

- Description of the securities?
- Aggregate par value?
- Terms and conditions of the option, agreement, or guarantee?

o. Customer account information which includes:

- Customer's name and residence or principal business address?
- Whether customer is of legal age?
- Occupation?
- Name and address of employer? And:
  - Whether customer is employed by a securities broker or dealer or by another municipal securities dealer?

- Name and address of beneficial owner or owners of the account if other than customer? And:
    - Whether transactions are confirmed with such owner or owners?
- Signature of municipal securities representative introducing the account?
- Signature of municipal securities principal accepting the account?
- With respect to discretionary accounts:
    - Customer's written authorization to exercise discretionary authority?
    - Written approval of the establishment of such account by the municipal securities principal who supervises the account?
    - Written approval by the supervising municipal securities principal for each transaction in the account, indicating the time and date of approval?
- Name and address of person(s) authorized to transact business for a corporate, partnership, or trusteed account? And:
    - Copy of powers of attorney, resolutions, or other evidence of authority to effect transactions for such an account? ✓
- With respect to borrowing or pledging securities held for the accounts of customers:
    - Written authorization from the customer authorizing such activities? ✓
- Customer complaints including:
    - Records of all written customer complaints?
    - Record of actions taken concerning those complaints?

p. Customer and the bank dealer's own account ledgers which include:

- All purchases and sales of securities?
- All receipts and deliveries of securities?
- All receipts and disbursements of cash?
- All other charges or credits?

q. Records of syndicates' joint accounts or similar accounts formed for the purchase of municipal securities which include:

- Underwriter agreements? And:

- Description of the security?
- Aggregate par value of the issue?
- Syndicate or selling group agreements? And:
  - Participants' names and percentages of interest?
  - Terms and conditions governing the formation and operation of the syndicate?
  - Date of closing of the syndicate account?
  - Reconcilement of syndicate profits and expenses?
- Additional requirements for syndicate or underwriting managers which include:
  - All orders received for the purchase of securities from the syndicate or account, except bids at other than the syndicate price?
  - All allotments of securities and the price at which sold?
  - Date of settlement with the issuer?
  - Date and amount of any good faith deposit made with the issuer?

r. Files which include:

- Advertising and sales literature? ✓
- Prospectus delivery information? ✓

s. Internal supervisory records which include:

- Personnel registration and investigation information? ✓
- Account reconcilement and follow-up? ✓
- Profit analysis by trader? ✓
- Sales production reports? ✓
- Periodic open position reports computed on a trade date or when issued basis? ✓
- Reports of own bank credit extensions used to finance the sale of trading account securities? ✓

23. Does the bank preserve the following municipal securities records for the periods of time indicated:

a. An itemized daily record of all purchases and sales, all receipts and deliveries of securities, all receipts and disbursements of cash, and all other debits and credits pertaining to municipal securities for 6 years?

b. Customer and bank dealer's own account ledgers for 6 years?

c. Customer complaint records for 6 years?

d. Customer account information relating to the opening and maintenance of the account for a period of at least 6 years following the closing of an account?

e. Securities position ledgers?

f. Records of syndicate transactions for 6 years? (Such records need not be preserved for an account that was not successful in purchasing an issue of municipal securities.)

g. Secondary records for 3 years which include:

- Transfer, validation, borrowed or loaned and fail ledgers or tickets?
- Put options and repurchase agreements?
- Records of principal and agency transactions (order tickets and confirmations)?
- Checkbooks, checking account statements, canceled checks, reconcilement, and wire transfers?
- Receivables and payables?
- All written communication received or sent, including inter-office memoranda, on the conduct of activities in municipal security transactions?
- All other customer account information?
- All other written agreements entered into with respect to any municipal securities account?

24. Are all records required to be preserved in a readily accessible place for at least 2 years, and thereafter, in a reasonably accessible place?

25. If records are preserved in any manner other than the original format of the record, does the bank have available facilities for ready retrieval, inspection and reproduction of legible facsimiles?

26. Has the bank officially designated at least one registered municipal securities principal to maintain and preserve records (if so, give name, _____)?

- Is a record of each such designation maintained showing the name, title, and business address of the person so designated and the date of designation?
- Is such a record retained for 6 years following any change in designation?

Purchase and Sales Transactions

27. Are all transactions promptly confirmed in writing to the actual customers or dealers?

28. Are confirmations compared or adequately tested to purchase and sales memoranda and reports of execution of orders, and any differences investigated and corrected (including approval by a designated responsible employee)?

   a. Are confirmations and purchase and sale memoranda checked or adequately tested for computation and terms by a second individual?

29. Are comparisons received from other dealers or brokers compared with confirmations, and any differences promptly investigated?

   a. Are comparisons approved by a designated individual (if so, give name _____)?

Customer and Dealer Accounts

30. Do account bookkeepers periodically transfer to different account sections or otherwise rotate posting assignments?

31. Are letters mailed to customers requesting confirmation of changes of address?

   a. Are confirmation requests mailed to both the customer's old and new address?

32. Are separate customer account ledgers maintained for:

- Employees?
- Affiliates?
- Own bank's trust accounts?

33. Are customer inquiries and complaints handled exclusively by designated individuals who have no incompatible duties?

34. Are written municipal securities customer account broker-to-broker transfers coordinated so that (MSRB rule G-26):

a. Upon receipt of a customer transfer instruction, the receiving party immediately submits the instruction to the carrying party?

b. The customer account carrying party within five business days validates and returns the instruction or takes exception to and advises the receiving party?

c. The customer account carrying party, within five business days of the validation, completes the transfer of the customer account?

d. The customer account receiving and carrying parties establish fail-to-receive and fail-to-deliver contracts on their books and institute the close-out procedures of rule G-12?

Other

35. Is the preparation, additions, and posting of subsidiary records performed and/or adequately reviewed by persons who do not also have sole custody of securities?

36. Are subsidiary records reconciled, at least monthly, to the appropriate general ledger accounts and are reconciling items adequately investigated by persons who do not also have sole custody of securities?

37. Are fails to receive and deliver under a separate general ledger control?

a. Are fail accounts periodically reconciled to the general ledger and any differences followed up to a conclusion?

b. Are periodic aging schedules prepared (if so, indicate frequency _____)?

c. Are stale fail items confirmed and followed up to a conclusion?

d. Are stale items valued periodically and, if any potential loss is indicated, is a particular effort made to clear such items or to protect the bank from loss by other means?

38. With respect to securities loaned and borrowed positions:

a. Are details periodically reconciled to the general ledger, and any differences followed up to a conclusion?

b. Are positions confirmed periodically (if so, indicate frequency _____)?

39. Is the compensation of all department employees limited to salary and a non-departmentalized bonus or incentive plan?

a. Are sales representatives' incentive programs based on sales volume or sales profit, and not department income?

Conclusion

40. Is the foregoing information an adequate basis for evaluating internal control in that there are no significant additional internal auditing procedures, accounting controls, administrative controls, or other circumstances that impair any controls or mitigate any weaknesses indicated above (explain negative answers briefly, and indicate conclusions as to their effect on specific examination or verification procedures)?

41. Based on a composite evaluation, as evidenced by answers to the foregoing questions, internal control is considered _____ (good, medium, or bad).

1. Test the additions of the inventory schedules and the reconciliation of the schedules to the general ledger.

2. Request that safekeeping agents, receiving and delivering parties of items in transit, and holders of loaned securities provide detailed lists of all securities held.

3. Using appropriate sampling techniques, select items from inventory schedules and perform the following:

    a. Prepare count slips indicating the quantity and description of the security.

    b. Determine which securities are:

        *   Held by the bank.
        *   Held by others.
        *   Held partially by the bank and partially by others.

    c. Indicate the location of securities held entirely by the bank or by others on the count slips.

    d. For securities held partially by the bank and partially by others:

        *   Indicate the quantity held by the bank on the count slip.
        *   Prepare additional count slips indicating the quantity held by others.

    e. Sort count slips by location.

    f. Number each set of count slips consecutively, and maintain a control record of the numbers used.

4. For those securities selected in step 3 which are held by the bank:

a. Physically examine and count the securities.

b. It physical count agrees with the count slip amount, initial the count slip.

c. If physical count does not agree with the count slip amount:

- Note the quantity actually counted.
- Request that bank personnel recount the security.
- If the discrepancy is resolved, initial the count slip.
- If the discrepancy is not resolved, initial the count slip, and request that bank personnel sign it.
- Give unresolved count slip discrepancies to the examiner controlling the count for follow-up and investigation.

5. For those securities selected in step 3 which are held by others:

a. Agree quantity as shown on safekeeping confirmation to count slip.

b. Investigate any discrepancies.

6. Account for all count slips, and:

a. Determine that all discrepancies have been satisfactorily resolved.

b. Discuss with management and prepare report comments on any unresolved discrepancies.

7. Using appropriate sampling techniques, select items from fails and due bills schedules, and:

a. Prepare and mail confirmation forms to customer(s). Confirmation forms should include a description of the security and the nature of the transaction, price, delivery date, and current balance.

b. Follow-up on any no-replies or exceptions and resolve differences.

8. Using appropriate sampling techniques, select items from good faith deposits and cash collateral schedules, and:

a. Prepare and mail confirmation forms to syndicate participants.

b. Follow-up on any no-replies or exceptions and resolve difference.

9. Test gains and losses on underwriting and trading account transactions since the last examination by selecting items from sales records, and:

a. Determining sales price by examining invoices or broker's advices.

b. Checking computation of book value on settlement date.

c. Calculating gain or loss.

d. Tracing gain or loss to proper recording in general ledger.

(Steps 10 and 11 should be performed only if the examiner-in-charge determines that it is necessary as an extension of similar computations made in NBSS reports.)

10. Obtain or prepare a schedule showing the accrued interest balances and the ending trading account balance for each quarter since the last examination, and:

a. Calculate quarterly ratio.

b. Investigate significant fluctuations and/or trends.

11. Obtain or prepare a schedule showing the monthly income amounts and the average securities balances for each month since the last examination, and:

a. Calculate monthly yield.

b. Investigate significant fluctuations and/or trends.